AF255661

Reckless Pilgrims

Reckless Pilgrims

Journeys to Faith

Thomas Sabel

RESOURCE *Publications* · Eugene, Oregon

RECKLESS PILGRIMS
Journeys to Faith

Resource Publications
An Imprint of Wipf and Stock Publishers
199 W. 8th Ave., Suite 3
Eugene, OR 97401

www.wipfandstock.com

PAPERBACK ISBN: 978-1-6667-7350-7
HARDCOVER ISBN: 978-1-6667-7351-4
EBOOK ISBN: 978-1-6667-7352-1

05/12/23

For Judith

Contents

Introduction

THE NOTION OF USING poetry to engage the world with the Gospel raises the question of how overt the poetry should be. Should it be didactic and systematic as well as apologetic? Should it promulgate the church's doctrine in poetic form? Such an approach would yield poetry that would fail to engage the world, but would remain within churchly confines, benefiting primarily the poet. Poetry is written for more than the poet (despite the tendency of current poetry that focuses on the poet's experience in the world expressed in strong emotions and intense subjectivity). The poet who strives to engage the world with the Gospel is in an odd situation that could quickly yield a false either-or dilemma wavering between didacticism and solipsism. A third option exists and should be followed. That third way begins with the vast amount of poetry found within the Bible, starting with Genesis 1:1, where the creation story is presented in language that is readily described as poetic, with the repetitions and rhythm that is foundational for all poetry. It continues throughout the Old Testament with the Psalms only a portion. The prophets are some of the strongest poets in Scripture. The New Testament brings the *Magnificat*, the *Beatitudes*, and other examples.

Outside of Scripture are countless examples of those who used their poetic skills to tell the story of the Gospel. These examples demonstrate the strength of the poetry to proclaim the Gospel in a narrative form that borders on the parables such as Dante's *Divine Comedy* or Milton's *Paradise Lost*. More modern poets such as T. S. Elliot, Scott Cairns, and others bring into our era those who express the faith in ways beyond the didactic or solipsistic.

Unfortunately, these poets are read by a select few for currently the poetic voice is seldom heard beyond the obvious hymnody. This raises a question that has been raised before—why are the arts so neglected in the church? One of the reasons could be fear, the fear of the creativity that flows from the arts. The artist is different from the craftsman in that the artist tends towards a greater freedom of expression. Artistic freedom seeks to find expression of what is difficult to express, such as the authentic spiritual anxiety that discomforts the pious or causes the hearer, in the case of poetry, to confront the faith in a different light, a light that shines into the dark recesses of the world. Connecting religion with artistic expression may well be as old as religion itself if we consider prehistoric cave paintings as part of an unknown ritual and the building of the Gobekli temple with its attendant carvings. The modern era (depending on when modernity began) worked to break the link between art and religion.

The poems being offered here have been written in the hopes of engaging with the world. They have been written as a witness to the journey faith engenders. In this light, they are not easy and present images that don't fit into tidy, pious categories. The intent is to express the reality of a believer's life without falling into platitudes and worn-out phrases. Some will find these too religious while others may find them lacking in proper piety. I offer them as a journey, or better, a pilgrimage that wrestles with the profoundly bewildering experience of being a Christian in a time when the Christian faith is, according to Charles Taylor, one option among many, or a time when the politics of the moment seems to pollute the faith beyond recognition. The hope is that they call the reader to a deeper understanding, one that connects on a level that reaches into the heart and gently nudges that heart in the direction of the Gospel.

The collection is divided into three sets. The first carries the reader through the movement of a longing doubt bordering on unbelief to a certainty of redemption found in Christ culminating in reckless joy. The second is a cross-cultural experiment that uses the Persian (and Islamic) form of the ghazal to present the

common Lutheran order of the Divine Service. The third reinter-
prets the hymn "Salvation unto Us Has Come" through the form
of the sestina.

$$— \text{I} —$$

Reckless Pilgrims

Reckless Pilgrims

We wander from shrine to shrine,
longing to see the martyr's bones,
calcified shatters that sliver pauseless wonder.

We've gone from hope to hope, clutching the apostle's
optimistic words of faith's finality that this life
might be as true as the next, and what we've done

matters somehow. The glass remains darkened,
and with squinting eyes we can't see
beyond the liminal words.

Why won't Jesus walk across our Galilee?
We'd sit in the bottom of the boat, our backsides wrinkled
from the water of the storm that slashes,
praying they won't bail us out.

Awaiting the Prophet

Streaks on the window lie and I follow,
believing in the rain that never comes. Shut
up in the heavens—God's curse until Elijah

shows up at the widow's door, calling
for the last bread and oil, "Bake me a cake."
Such is the arrogance of the prophets,

such are the rules of hospitality.
Without a choice, they both obey
lest the world collapse to anarchy.

Or so they believe—nobody bothered to test
the rules until after the Greeks had their day
and the doubts took root, cracking foundations.

I look past the lies staining the window,
scanning the view. No sign of any Elijah.

The Infinity of Worry

You'd create worries out of dust mites
or pocket lint if God didn't provide them.
Each breath awaits the inhaling of problems
that fill your frantic air with the energy
of the distraught. Sisyphus had an easy time
with only a single task—the damned rock
upon an equally damned hill. That's Hades—
this is earth, bound by the multiplier effect
of quantum physics and universal parallels
of an infinite number of worries that spin
threads through neurons of your brain
until all creation floods the synapse
with hopeless trials of control. Dark matter
doesn't care. Why strain the effort
when the mites and lint trust God?

The Hand of God

"Too late schmart," my mother said,
drawling "sch" in theatrical German
lifted from the radio of her youth.
Lessons arrive after the need
and we scratch communal heads
at duplicitous stupidity—
we'll get it right next time.
I have a torrent of doubts
proving my insanity while making
the same mistake for God knows
how many times—if He keeps track,
shaking the head we've put on Him
to make Him more accessible,
like the way we give Him a voice
and ears and eyes and hand
in the singular, "The hand of God."
A hand with an infinity of fingers
to track our dumbness.
I wish He'd make a fist
to take it all away.

A Hymn to the Pacific Gyre

I.

I treat my body less than a temple;
a temple should be tidy—at least
clean shaven, unpolluted by the toxins
I delight in, the common market
toxins laid open on the altar of the liver,
kidneys, heart, and bowels (Praise be bowels!).
Holy libations, how I suffer open-throated
drain pipes, desecrated by abusive
horrors of the shattering wine glass.

Spirit, can You live within my detritus,
making a home among the littering pollution?
Clear a spot with the wide sweep of holy wings
and nestle upon the shelving.

II.

All the wine, all the cars, all the cell phones,
or other blessed technology (Hosanna to the microchip!).
Oozing streams from moribund oil wells,
petrochemicaling us into new creations.
Microscopic plastic beads float in our water, our air,
our bodies, mutating us into hydrocarbon
chains of permanence. What need for God when eternity
flows nanopiece by nanopiece in the blood,
collecting in the liver, that prophetic organ first to go.

"Roll me over in the clover and frack me" is the hymn
we sing, embracing the horizontal drill points
like St. Teresa clutches ecstatic darts of Christ.
Make us true believers while our pores bear witness
to doubters bound for holy decay.

Clutching the Dark

When the light bulb blows, I leave it.
The bulb's death may be the hand of God,
and darkness equals destiny laid down
before creation and the first light.
Changing it would ripple the chaos of butterflies,
hurricaning destruction, and I'd get blamed.
My fault, one more layer of blackened guilt
I get to wear, an iron-clad shawl
that sucks the warmth off my shoulders
as darkness swallows the sparks of remaining light
and the room enters the grave with unseen shadows
pinning the dawn like a wrestler
to the mat of useless tomorrows.

Thudding through Tomorrow

Yesterday closed his box with a thudding dullness
that escaped the ears of another room; ears
caught the tumult of tomorrow, not knowing

the stillborn traits of repetition—"Same old
same old," the aged like to say, squawking out
experience like newfound wisdom, astounded

over the prophetic voice clutching throats
in a final clasping of expression before the second
day has passed away, the trail of grave clothes.

How we'd relive those shuttering days, so we say,
voicing lies the ancestors spoke when they
passed on mistakes for us to catch in pools

opened by the mutant twist of destiny,
bearing the plan of God that lies a finger width
away from touching—a foretaste

of Zeno's arrow that never reaches its mark.
The eternal "almost," thudding . . .
thudding . . . thudding . . .

Terra Firma

Why know the world only as the cross
quickly cast off with welcome,
sighing the soul at the locking of the casket?
Born to suffer and die—what dismal sermons
despise the living and long for death's cure.
What nonsense to hold what God called good
like soiled rags of snot cast away
by legions of tubercular demons. That's where
your life might be found if you'd pick it up
and like Francis, kiss the wounds of the leper.

Why drag yourself in the opium of Gnostic tales?
The keys of connection
bind, and link, and chain you to the earth:
the blessed land of milk and honey, of bread and broiled onions,
flannel by winter's fire, and the wine. Never forget
the wine that bears comely burdens.
And God called it good.

Wallowing Obituary

I wallow in my pity, hollowing out
an empty niche for a statue
nobody bothered to carve—why
waste the stone on another gone bust?

I shouldn't read the shadowing obits
while worrying their lexicon of common
phrases that drain the life from the dead
into dirty plastic pails of banality.

The reported dead return to infantdom,
where all are innocent and blessed:
"loved his family, his god, his team."
With such perfection they should
bypass dying, like Enoch,
who walked with God and was no more.

I don't love sports and my family
pissed me off more than once. God
and I are still discussing guilt and shame,
wondering who has claim to what.

My wallowing keeps me busy
for another hollow day.

I Will Die of Broken Midnight

For Cesar Vallejo

I will die of broken midnight
when a sallow moon pulls the neap
tide of light from my telluric side.

I will die ready for breakage,
a cracked cup or mug or teapot
crackled with stains of words.

I will die of pulpit and conflictions,
the swelling of convictions
compounded with an overactive doubt.

They will bury me under words
spoken by strangers
bearing putrid dichotomies.

The Impossibility of the Jesus Poem

Begins with the mystery of hows—
how to believe,
how to love,
how to feel,
how to believe, again the how
returns to face the world
Jesus entered and brought hows.
How to be born once, then twice,
how to live last yet first,
how to love that rascal neighbor
who's howless about his life,
and you're supposed to love but can't stand
the S.O.B.
How again, to live like Christ
has entered your marrow.

To die—how? Always death
howling how on the cross
should this have happened?
Howling at the Father's abandonment.
How to let the pain take over—
unhealed, the healer dies.

How recorded in dead language;
how dissected words eviscerate.
How to find the holy,
how to pray for the hows
of possibility?

Seeking Timeless Worship

Seeking timeless worship,
lurching from church to church,
drunk
on the hope that this time
I'll be wrenched from time-bound worries,
set free into God's timeless elements.
Songs of angels not bound
by time
wrench me from the clocks that grind
by their gears.
Free from past or present or yet to come,
I'll sing the ancient grown new and—
now melds into yet to be.
I'll take the cup of Christ—
His blood flowing forever—
and drink, never ceasing
to flood my timeless being.

To "Truly Lent"

This year—I hope it's truer than last
when I didn't make it to Easter.
My forty days maybe got to ten,
depending on how generous the count,
and who made forty the magic number, God?
I'd like to know why not a lesser number,
like six or two. Jesus held out for forty,
setting the bar for the rest of us,
and some ancient yokel thought we should too.
The idea stuck to the church like fly specks
on the wall and can't get rid of it—
a constant reminder of what I hoped to do,
for God's sake, but usually don't.
Lent's all about forgiveness.

Cracking Lenten Skins

Lent brings catharsis, but not the kind expected,
not the purging from the bowels of sin
and plunging out the cloaca of hell,
a quick evacuation into the secret heavenlies
of Jesus. Lent is slow—a scrubbing of layers
that cling with claws. I've worn them so long
they've become a second, a third, a fourth skin—
protection against the flesh living beneath them;
flesh of freedom from the shielding shame,
living and vital, flesh and bone like Jesus
took from the womb of Mary, called "good" by God
from the beginning of goodness that still remains.
If only I could crack the skins and let it out,
despite the pain each fault line gives.
Lent bring catharsis—the groaning of mourning
the death of my shameful skins.

Θαρσις (Courage and Healing)

"Be healed." "Have courage." The word goes
both ways as Luke gives it in the Greek;
but Jesus didn't speak Greek—
I'll hang on it though—courage heals the timid
heartbeats of the sojourning spirit
that hopes to wander to the magic
some call heaven, others hell.
It's not that different
from vacation magazines that beckon
paradise from Indiana's March
of sleet and rain and mud
refusing to warm or dry, relentless
in its courage to cling to winter
before spring, like love
heals all things.

Being afraid is the easy way out, the quilt of paralysis
that wraps certainty even in summer
while sweat stains the pattern,
white streaks of salt faint against the flowers.
Sweating out fear like a fever never works;
the sickness remains.

Courage heals the sickness,
and the lame got up and walked,
and the blind saw sights that terrified
when darkness turned to light,
flooding the brain with new grace.

Jesus' Diner

When Jesus ate with sinners, He didn't count
calories or carbs. Being God, He knew about them,
along with sodium, transfats, and other nutrition
label data we mortals believe and trust in.

When Jesus dined with sinners, the Pharisees read
the labels of the guests to find them lacking
ingredients proper for the table, unlike Jesus.
The supper is holy when Jesus comes to eat,
savoring His Father's gifts without modern chemistry
splintering the meal into competing factions.

When Jesus dines with sinners, will He teach us
proper manners of breaking forth the Father's bread
along with meat and wine like Isaiah's ancient promise?
God's mealtide gifts enrich despite our counting.

When Jesus dined with sinners, He bore
the label of drunkard like He'd bear the cross.

I miss the meals that Jesus ate.

Thursday's Table Prayer

Love the food for food is good declares
the Lord when He sits down with sinners
like me. The common Lutheran table prayer
invites, "Come, be our guest."
Words rattle from salivating lips like
the Russian dog, not wondering if the prayer
is heard and Jesus shows up. We'll ignore
Him, just the same as we always do a stranger
who shows up at the table, making us nervous.
We pretend we're other than we are; polite
like Judas, minding our words before
they betray raw truth served as a salad
with the first course, an embarrassment
that reveals us to our heavenly guest
when dessert is served and our sweetness
overwhelms the coarseness of the meal.

Good Friday I

We're not searching for joy,
but dealing with pain,
the simple, common, and boring
aches of the spirit that dull
the presence of God who's supposedly
all over the place and shares our grief
like He took our share to the cross
that the Romans drove
into the navel of the world,
like the festering splinter
your mother can't remove
and the redness swells out,
serving up the tender spot
fought over for a thousand years.
No passing peace here
that would numb the pain
that follows the draining
search for a joy scattered
like the blood on four horns
of the altar from the splintering
wound caused by Roman pride.

Good Friday II

Better to look away, turn from the violence—
pretend it isn't there,
like we do with other abuse close to home.
Wear corpus-free crosses of jewels
to catch the sunlight, not noontime's darkness
of Good Friday that shatters dreams
of death-free living.
"Pick up your cross," Jesus said. "We're all going to die."
Ever the realist who knew both sides of the coin
the thief stole and the soldiers coveted.
"Pick up your cross." A lonely way,
like Jesus alone in the middle of the crowd
milling around like a picnic at lynch time.
"Pick up your cross." Join Jesus at the place
that's hard to say
and gets stuck in the throat,
too bitter to swallow.
"Pick up your cross."

Saturday's Leftovers

Sun lies, "Morning," to half-shut idealism,
calling from blessed-out hopes
built on nothing less than the bloody mess
of another's leftover agony.
The pain thrust open-dished
into the refrigerator three days
old, dried, beyond restitution.
Saran wrap's salvation could have saved
the hopeful dream if only enshrouded in time.
Old Joe of Arimathea failed to show up,
likewise the three Marys and the apostolic gang.
They switched sandals out for boots on Harleys
and thundered West, escaping the rising sun;
searching for other leather-backed angels,
and leaving you to find the truth
in the bare sheets of unyielding day.

Sunday's Child

The poem refuses to budge off
its groove, like the stone
in front of Jesus' tomb.
I talk like the Marys,
"Who will roll the stone away?"
But no angels fly in to shoulder
the poem on its way—
my wingless weight
will have to do, so I lean
into the poem and shove.
Whole words, like gravel dust,
tumble from the top, a sign
of headway, ever so small,
until the poem starts to roll
off the groove and down
the hill that hides the tomb
filled with angel feathers
that fly my freedom.

Dancing in the Meadow

He leads, of course, shows
the steps with cross-earned
grace. I follow, stumbling on
Judas-feet betraying
His calm choreography.

He forgives the times I
trod His nail-bruised feet,
slight smiles embrace my clumsiness,
pushing past my broken steps.
"Don't try, just follow."

Before I joined in Jesus' dance
meadow weeds pricked my soles—
a thousand shards of pain
driving me from the field.

But now, unleashed, I go
into His flow and leave
awkward mis-stepped days
of trudging the endless trail.
Feet grown light kiss the grass
leaving blades unbruised, unbent.

The spheres sing Kepler's tune
as we waltz across the meadow.
The Easter sun stretches shadows
long past our vision's sight.

—— II ——

Lutheran Ghazals

ACCORDING TO AGHA SHAHID Ali, the ghazal is an ancient form of Persian poetry composed of autonomous or semiautonomous couplets united by a strict pattern of rhyme, refrain, and line length. "One couplet may be comic, another tragic, another romantic, another religious, another political."[1] The first couplet establishes the pattern by having it in both lines, and then it appears in the second line of each succeeding couplet. The final couplet includes a signature, that is, the name of the poet. These ghazals strive to be true to the form while simultaneously reflecting a Lutheran ethos.

The arrangement of the ghazals follows that of the traditional order of service found in many Lutheran congregations on a given Sunday.

1. Ali, *Ravishing Disunities.*

Confession

The members sang, "Lord, to You I Make Confession"
then spent the week working to break confession.

She sat (see her shyness) in the long-empty pew.
The final hymn revealed (feel her ache) confession.

Pope Urban roiled at Luther's Thesis
knowing what was at stake: confession.

Because they believed in waterboarding's surety,
the CIA trusted the Taliban's fake confession.

The weight of God's Law collapsed their pride;
they begged, "Pastor Sabel, please take confession."

Kyrie

"The truth will set you free," says Jesus,
and whatever the price, pays Jesus.

With water from heaven, rolling down the mountain
and upon the ground, John the Baptist sprays Jesus.

The party ended hours ago. Longing for bed,
I cleaned the room and who still stays? Jesus.

What is worse, ending up hung on the cross
or in Walmart—a candy-headed Pez Jesus?

Her prayer is so God-awful important that she
fret and moans and cries as she delays Jesus.

Believers' hearts refused to budge when
finally they found, "Here Lies Jesus."

Mountains shivered the tiniest bit each time
Thomas, hearing the call, prays, "Jesus."

Scripture Readings

Through Easter the Resurrected One is crowned in the readings
but many still find the story unsound in the readings.

The monotonous tone from the quavering lectern
sent waves of sleep that drowned in the readings.

Doctors and nurses studied the patient's chart
for a sign that health would rebound in the readings.

Everything else had failed. The old woman leaned
in leery hope to have her guilt unbound in the readings.

On Sunday, the voice of most prophets is seldom heard
because their words only confound in the readings.

When anguish wrenched Brother Martin's heart,
he heard the howl of Heaven's Hound in the readings.

In Monopoly, the player who picks the right card
will be lucky in the ride found on the Reading.

"The tarot can't lie," said the fortune teller.
"You'll find love renowned in the readings."

We've heard it before in dull repetition. Why the surprise
when familiarity fails to astound in the readings?

Thomas scoured the library's shelves, clutching books to make his empty soul rebound in the readings.

32

Hymn of the Day

The Bridegroom soon will call—He marries through eternity.
Sing with all the saints God's glories through eternity.

Oh, Gentle One, even across a thousand miles
the touch of your lips lingers and carries through eternity.

Come follow me, the Savior spake , and we went,
trusting His promise of rest and peace through eternity.

"I'm finished with you forever," she said, throwing her lovers
away. She wouldn't want more of these through eternity.

Constricted by His first creation, God flung wide
the word of the universe and with ease threw eternity.

Born and raised in Indiana's woodlands, Pastor Sabel
feared living out his life on the prairies through eternity.

Sermon

Medieval monks' self-made perfection trounced grace alone.
Brother Martin struggled to hear announced—grace alone.

Wearing unquenchable piety, they forced their Jesus—
prideful in forgiveness, they flounced grace alone.

Two theological athletes took to the court
and off each other's doctrine bounced grace alone.

How surprised I was when freed from the confines
of her clothes, in bliss-born nudity, bounced Grace alone.

Listen, Thomas, you'll scarce believe your ears;
your freedom's come, the heavens pronounced grace alone.

The Creed

From their daily work the apostles were called to believe;
anxious parents throw kids in the car and hauled to believe.

Like unconcerned fisherfolk, some seekers lack wisdom,
cast wide undiscerned nets and trawled to believe.

The superstitious robed midwife exclaimed to the mother,
"Not only six toes and a tail, this child's cauled too. Believe!"

The pressure of the Series must have shattered the pitcher.
He threw wide then broke and balked two—believe.

With images of hell meticulously described, Savonarola,
by force of wind, the Florentines would scold to believe.

When the Beloved explained they could meet no more,
Thomas, finally broken in spirit, bawled to believe.

The Prayers

Lenten Pilgrims clutched hands to offer prayer
that God would once again suffer prayer.

Charlene lay shattered between lilac sheets
while bruised lungs tried to cough up prayer.

In hapless attempt to unlock God's ear
they twisted holy words to doctor prayer.

Tattered refugees combined in worship,
then laid in the open coffer—prayer.

When asked how she knew his unbroken pain,
the sister smiled to her brother, "Prayer."

Made roofless by the hurricane's wrenching,
the church stayed open for another prayer.

Longing for evening, Thomas caught the sunset
when he crossed the yard for Vesper prayer.

The *Sanctus*

Deafening glories of angelic voices din heaven and earth.
Isaiah straddled beyond hope in heaven and earth.

What was it, again, that God planned to restore
when all was shattered by sin? Heaven and earth.

All our wrangling, all our bickering, does little more
than turn creation into a has-been heaven and earth.

Borge's Aleph left the Argentinean basement
To dwell in an Indiana oats bin—heaven and earth.

The empty tomb, the hollow shroud, while angelic light
shattered the barrier between heaven and earth.

"Thomas," my Beloved, tonguing my ears, whispers,
"This time our love will set to quaking heaven and earth."

The *Pax Domini*

Jesus stole Passover's table to conceal body and blood,
leavenless bread and sweet kosher wine the seal—body and blood.

The church tore at her guts in hapless bantering
over the concept as slippery as an eel: body and blood.

Heaven-seeking Christians trip, stumble, and fall
when they forget that life is real body and blood.

Imprisoned by magic, priests locked the elements away
to stop uncouth peasants who sought to steal body and blood.

Centurions knew Jesus' whole death. This lead them
to gamble and squeal, "such a deal, body and blood!"

To punish the sailor they dragged the poor man,
dismembered to pieces from under the keel, body and blood.

To the altar I drag my death-stenched carcass.
Enliven me by Your holy gift that heals—body and blood.

Bored with the preaching and driven by the clock's call
half the congregation woke when the bell pealed "Body and Blood."

We split heaven from earth to keep the spiritual safe
and now we think God should repeal body and blood.

Holy Supper, kiss my sin-bearing lips.
Cleanse Thomas when You reveal body and blood.

Agnus Dei

Jesus refused Gethsemane's choice to go on the lam of God
and instead went to Calvary to bleed out the Lamb of God.

Eve and Adam should have taken a practical bent,
killed the snake, and cooked up jellies and jam of God.

The boastful sinner prays the certainty that in the end
will be heard by all the final "scram!" of God.

When Jesus cast the demon into the herd,
pigs rejoiced and plunged off the cliff—the ham of God.

Too many hurl verses like artillery shells
until the Bible becomes the spam of God.

Despite attempts to strip her of honors,
Mary remains the highly favored dame of God.

Caught in a sniggering adolescence, Noah's youngest
tattled and became the cursed Ham of God.

St. Peter, in Western garb, opened the Pearly Gates
for the Woman of Wyoming saying, "Yes, Ma'am, of God."

Cursed with modern impatience, Thomas sits anxiously
waiting to hear the vibrant *I Am* of God.

Holy Communion

The Son of God. How could this be the Christ for you?
Angelic soldiers drain the body and fill the chalice for you.

Dressed in rags and left to flounder, the angels welcome.
Discover all this beauty, all this palace for you.

Remember the butterfly. Take your suffering, wrap it
around. This life is but a chrysalis for you.

The fruit picked from the golden tree of Paradise—
the Beloved stole from the pie a slice for you.

Motherless, soulless evil stalks you in light
and in darkness bearing only malice for you.

You seek the labyrinth through the rabbit hole?
Find her, the young virgin Alice for you.

The fever struck; your body's burning. Clutch
this, Tommie, the bag of healing ice for you.

Benediction

The choir director struggled with tenors to sing a new song.
With long-tired ears, the pastor prayed they'd bring a new song.

Like a cow drunk on fermented mash, last night's wine
made me curious, so I was ruminating a new song.

Too many years, too many sorrows left him bleeding.
Alone in the end, he had a hard time believing a new song.

Ah, my Beloved, are we left merely with memories
of when we spent the night caressing a new song?

In unlutheran fashion, the members sat up in the pews,
in full-throated rapture began rejoicing—a new song!

Now, Thomas, you've come to the end—
is anything left to help you cling to a new song?

—— III ——

Sestinas on
Salvation unto Us Has Come

Sᴇsᴛɪɴᴀs ᴀʀᴇ ᴀ ꜰᴏʀᴍ of poetry invented by the ancient French troubadours and they tend to be more narrative than lyrical. "A sestina has six unrhymed stanzas of six lines each in which the words at the ends of the first stanza's lines recur in a rolling pattern at the ends of the other lines. The sestina then concludes with a tercet (three-line stanza) that also uses all six end-words, two to a line."[1]

These sestinas use the hymn, "Salvation unto Us Has Come" by Paul Speratus (1484–1551), as a stepping-off point or a prompt to develop a confession of faith. This collection offers one sestina per stanza and follows the curve, the theological line of discussion. They seek to probe into and beneath the lines of the stanzas, revealing an existential pilgrimage from death to eternal life in Christ.

In the following poems the six words that are used in the sestinas are set in bold-faced type in the hymn verse. Those words create the pattern.

1. Padgett, *Teachers and Writers Handbook.*

Sestina One

Salvation unto us has come
*By God's **free grace** and favor;*
*Good works cannot avert out **doom**,*
They help and save us never.
***Faith** looks to Jesus Christ **alone**,*
*Who did for all the **world** atone;*
He is our one Redeemer.

We swore we needed all this to not be free
from carrying it. We loved our baggage that we grace-
lessly hauled from one place to another—a doom
written in unseen ledgers escribed so faith-
fully by drones who labored on alone
in disconnected unity; somewhere in the world

we believed we knew so well. We travel the world,
you and I, hoping to express hard-won free-
dom until we realized that we were never alone
in our persistent pursuit of the gentle grace
that would smile on our struggles. Ah, faith!
Why are you so elusive? Must we face our doom

with smiling faces, ignoring the oppressive doom
of choices made by others? We avoid dreaming a world
where hope skips hand in hand with faith
facing the challenges that halt our free
choice. Should we ever gain the grace
to toss the baggage? Let it float alone

down whatever river flows alone
through the avid dreams, doom-
ing the restless travels propelling us grace-
lessly past the ebb and flow of one world
and onto the next? Our tickets aren't free,
or so we believed, bought with full faith

and credit. We shouldn't put all our faith
in some private destination we alone
can see, deluded that we might not be free
and while home, refusing to see that doom
for what it is; pained by a world
not of our dreams. Likely, we lack the grace

to tear the blindness off our eyes. Such grace
has never been part of us, nor has the faith
to reveal the ways of an unmasked world.
And so, we drag our luggage alone,
down long crowded corridors to a doom
we dreamed would set us free.

Lacking the grace to leave luggage alone
and without the faith to face our doom,
the world's chains keep us from being free.

Sestina Two

*What God did in the Law **demand***
And none to Him could render
*Caused **wrath** and woe on every hand*
*For man, the **vile** offender.*
*Our **flesh** has not those pure **desires***
*The **spirit** of the Law requires*
And lost is our condition.

The day I waken into makes the demand
of doing—Accomplish! Get it done lest wrath
fall upon me, exposing me for the vile
creature I am. I find I've little desire
to move much further from the bed. The flesh
says stay where you are—let pass the spirit

of the age that beckons only labor. Then the spirit
calls full-bore, making a distant demand
that I rise from sloth to earn my pound of flesh
before being exposed to the persistent wrath
that pollutes even the commonplace desire.
Rising, I leave the bed unmade, a vile

collection of tossed-about bedding that carry the vile
dreams which dissipate in the form of a spirit
that refuses recollection, despite my desire
to call it back as the day drags the demand
to join the rest of the pack before the wrath
falls. Together we strive to push the flesh

beyond its tarnished limits, to flesh
out the day, to find meaning beyond the vile
churnings that are so filled with wrath
that fires the belly like a burning spirit.
What life is this, forcing the constant demand
to fulfill the emptiness of the desire

which leaves unmet any sort of desire
other than the simple feeding of the flesh?
Oh, that I could halt and make my demand,
my moment of rebellion against the face of vile
commitment to a cause unblessed. My spirit
lacks such fortitude and weakly I accept the wrath

that pummels me into submission. This wrath
cracks like a whip, a goad that desires
to drive me on, hoping to breathe the spirit
as well as destroy my exhausted flesh
until I collapse into a worn-out pile of vile
contempt, strengthless against its demand.

The weighted pounds of wrath press bruised flesh
past the hope of desire, leaving a taste so vile
the spirit can't swallow it, broken by demands.

Sestina Three

*It was **false**, misleading **dream***
That God His Law had given
That sinners could themselves redeem
*And by their works gain **heaven**.*
*The Law is but a **mirror** bright*
*To bring our **inbred** sin to light*
*That **lurks** within our nature.*

Betrayal came under the guise of a false
friend—the sort who dangles a dream
of a shortcut that sounds like heaven
to itching ears. Check the cracked mirror
and find between the shards the inbred
thought that betrays the thing lurking

in the gray lines that thread and lurk,
bearing contemptible power of the falsehood
driving and coercing every inbred
move seeking perfection—it's a dream,
the sort that lingers in morning's mirror,
starring back through a darkened heaven.

The studies flow on, eagerly pointing to a heaven
gained through newfound rules. Behind them lurks
the hope, the desire, that denies the mirror's
unrelenting truth. Wherein lies the false,
misplaced goal of a perfection only dreamed
by sellers of goods? Such notions are inbred

into the soul, unable to escape the inbreeding
that lives within, cutting heaven
off, leaving it as a remorseless dream,
forgotten from long neglect. Its staleness lurks
in faint shadows that cower like false
images, half-seen before the mirror's

reflection. Could another be seen in the mirror?
Or could the illusion be so inbred
that freedom remains beyond the grasp, a false
goal based on the absurdity of a hoped-for heaven
when all that remains is what still lurks
within, without—while the attempt to cast a dream

of another sort falters. Left without a dream,
all that remains are the lies of the mirror
that linger and laugh, joining the lurking
illusion that refused to go—inbred
into the painful longing for a heaven
proven to be disappointingly false.

Such a dream creates the inbred
hope that belies the mirror's glimpse of heaven
that remains lurking, calling all else false.

Sestina Four

*From **sin** our flesh could not abstain,*
*Sin held its sway **unceasing;***
*The **task** was useless and in **vain**,*
Our guilt was e'er increasing.
*None can remove sin's **poisoned** dart*
*Or **purify** our guileful heart—*
So deep is our corruption.

I'm falling—still falling since sin
pushed me over the edge. This unceasing
tumbling over and over. Lost is the task
of trying to improve. It's all in vain
and slowly I realize the poison
that flows through my veins. Why purify

what is beyond cleansing? Stop the purifying
madness. Accept the truth of sin,
that it's a slow-working poison
pulsing decay in an unceasing
manner. Realize fully how vain
is the uselessness of the task.

Give it all up, I say; toss the task
of betterment into the trash. Let it purify
the garbage if it can. Grow vain
instead, bloated with courageous sin
and stalk the world with unceasing
pride, spreading destructive poison

with broad laughter, oozing out the poison
that infects everyone who takes the task
of betterment upon themselves. Unceasing
is this newfound goal—to purify
the world of purification. Now let sin
rule! Indulge temptations! See how vain

we all can be! All is vanity, vanity.
And that's the point. As the poison
festers, the stench of gangrenous sin
fills the air, fulfilling its task
of spreading decay. Acrid aromas purify
out fresh scents of hope. Unceasingly

it embraces the world. With unceasing
amusement I realize at last how vain
and empty we all have become. I can't purify
the filth so I drink down the poison,
longing for the end, closing off the task
of living—graving myself with sin.

Embrace the unceasing flow of poison,
realizing, at last, how vain remains the task.
Nothing purifies; I grin death's final sin.

Sestina Five

Yet as the Law must be fulfilled
*Or we must **die** despairing,*
*Christ came and has God's **anger** stilled,*
*Our human **nature** sharing.*
*He has for us the Law **obeyed***
*And thus the Father's **vengeance** stayed*
*Which over **us** impended.*

Listen to me—is the best we can do is die?
Where is the justice? Seething with anger,
are we left bereft, only to follow our nature,
join the rest of creation, called to obey
the rule of decay? Why not seek vengeance
against the giver of laws who condemned us

to this pitiful state? Our striving made us
hollow, filled with the desire to live, not die.
Our failure to follow erupts with His vengeance,
His judgment. Through imperfection His anger
is rightly earned in failed attempts to obey.
We'd rather steal His throne—it's our fallen nature.

Left without hope, we slowly see that all nature
joins us in this march to corruption, united with us.
The world becomes an open grave that obeys
the call to swallow life. Finally stung, all dies.
We've longed to flee from the brunt of anger
that envelops with inescapable vengeance.

But look! One comes, embracing the vengeance.
Though the pain is great, one of us with a second nature,
the same but different, who takes in all the anger
that's aimed directly, pointedly upon us
as if He owned it all, letting Himself die
for those who cared not, hearing the call to obey

in a way that we never heard. He hears, obeys,
keeps every rule we broke and halts the vengeance
we rightly gained. No more must we die,
or fear the wrath due our corrupted nature.
What a surprise He is; He loves us
into Himself, and so frees us from the anger

of divine destruction. No more the brunt of anger,
we rejoice and dance a newfound tune that obeys
an unearthly rhythm. What's left for us?
To abandon the threat of vengeance,
to revel in our newborn nature,
casting into the abyss the fear of dying.

What once raised our anger and longing for vengeance
is laid upon He who obeys and through His holy nature
has embraced us into life, no more to die.

Sestina Six

*Since Christ has **full** atonement made*
And brought to us salvation,
*Each Christian therefore must be **glad***
*And **builds** on this foundation.*
Your grace alone, dear Lord, I plead,
*Your **death** is now my **life** indeed,*
*For You have paid my **ransom**.*

The glass once parched to bone sits full
and more—life overflows in glad
delight; the heart once stone now builds
on new-grown hope that shatters death
and quickens the marrow to dance the life
unknown. How great the surprise that ransoms

out of long-feared decay—paying a ransom
exceeding imagination. Beyond count, the full
cost, once so high it demanded a holy life;
one enters, pure and uncorrupt, gladly
giving Himself over to the call of death
undeserved yet necessary. How do I build

on such a beginning? What seems unjust builds
upon a plan I can't comprehend—the ransom
required since nearly the beginning, of a death,
of a sacrifice so great it took the fullness
of God to make it. From love, He is glad
to do it so that I and others can enter life

and gain the longed-for glimpse of life
as first intended when God set about to build
the world. Were I to say I'm glad,
that wouldn't be enough. The joy of being ransomed
is too great to tell. A heart more that full,
stretches to exploding, bringing a death

of all that was—the suffering embrace of death
as answer. Here arrived an undeserved life,
the sort I never dreamed, one so full
it must overflow—a newborn way to build
in answer to the call that came with ransom
paid, expressing gratitude with a gladness
rising dawn-like, with a freshness that gladdens
the heart stripped of the fear of death,
eager to run in the love that flows from a ransomed
soul. What adventure awaits in this life
freely given—an enduring gift to build
an everlasting joy that's never completely full.

The gladdened heart rejoices in the life
that conquered death and opened the way to build
upon the ransom paid. The glass is full.

Sestina Seven

*Let me not **doubt**, but truly see*
*Your word cannot be **broken**;*
*Your call **rings** out, "Come unto Me!"*
No falsehood have You spoken.
*Baptized into Your **precious name**,*
My faith cannot be put to shame,
*And I shall never **perish**.*

Joy dissipates when the stench of decay raises doubt
and I wonder if the promises have been broken
like so many I've known. The truth that rings
can sound so hollow and I question the precious
value of the gift given. His valuable name
loses its sweetness and I fear I'll perish

in the abyss I scorned before, neglecting that He perished
for me, absolving away the abyss, gathering doubt
into Himself. Into the purity of His name
he bathed me—a flood of grace that has broken
the old to shatters. Yet, that old still has precious
grasp. It tries to entice, draw rings

around me, luring me away, dangling rings
and pretty things, all the stuff that will perish.
Like a blinding light in an endless cave, His precious
word loves out the despair, making doubt
flee like some blackened hollow; broken
is the shadowing power. By His will His name

I claim, He poured it over me. The true name,
written before time began—the one that rings
true—that's good, right, and proper—not broken
beyond repair. Had I held the old, I'd perish
at the end. As with my sin, He claims my doubt
and in love exchanges it with His precious

body and blood, the greatest gift made precious
through humility. To invoke His name
is to bring His presence that throws all doubt
outside creation's boundary. His word rings
out and sounds the alarm to all who perish.
Why ponder on the world that's broken

when you know He paid for it with His broken
body? The faith He gave is more precious
than silver or gold because it will never perish,
while I cling to the priceless gift of His name,
secure in His loving embrace. Rings
of grace surround, removing the decay of doubt.

Taken from the broken world and bathed into His name,
I become more precious to Him than all the rings
of power. Through Him I perish not and cast aside all doubt.

Sestina Eight

*The Law **reveals** the guilt of sin*
And makes us conscience stricken;
*But then the Gospel **enters** in*
*The sinful **soul** to quicken.*
*Come to the cross, **trust** Christ, and live;*
*The Law no **peace** can ever give,*
*No comfort and no **blessing.***

What has been shown so far reveals
an impossibility painfully freighted that enters
what we perceive; that a self-striving soul
is doomed to torment. The misplaced trust
offers nothing and the longed-for peace
retreats farther and farther off. No blessing

here, only the abyss. The word of blessing
comes from without, a great surprise that reveals
the unlikely place, the foolish plan of peace
that we would never develop. By stealth it enters
through the gentle obedience of a girl who trusts
the angelic word and gives herself—soul

and body—an instrument to bring to souls
the cure for their cursed state, a blessing
beyond all reckoning, and unbreakable trust
from the creator who chose the time to reveal
the closing of time as eternity enters.
Life now reigns, not death, and peace

enlivens the once dead who sing, "Peace
in our time oh send us." Harried souls
find rest when His hope-filled words enter
the ears and nestle in the heart. Blessing
flows in cleansing torrents that reveal
the sought-for mystery. A lively trust

cleaves tightly to an instrument of death, trusting
in the outpoured blood, the sacrifice of peace
that scorns all dying. Faith reveals
the cost of freedom birthing a soul
now sinless and alive. Freshly found blessings
flow in, abounding astounds as they enter,

opening unforeseen horizons. A wholeness enters
empty of striving. Gone is the need to trust
in the self. That's all behind, replaced by a blessing
of life made whole, and what remains is the peace
delivered, otherworldly that grounds the soul
on the unshakable hope finally revealed.

From the far outside there enters what brings peace,
exceeding my trust; He calls my soul
to follow the blessings into all He reveals.

Sestina Nine

*Faith **clings** to Jesus' **cross** alone*
*And **rests** in Him unceasing;*
*And by its **fruits** true faith is known,*
*With love and **hope** unceasing.*
For faith alone can justify;
Works serve our neighbor and supply
*The proof that faith is **living**.*

Doubts still fly and they try to cling
like burrs on matted fur. They long to cross
the line, dragging along the rest
of the backsliders, returning to pick the fruit
that fed the first corruption, stealing the hope
graciously given, staining the gift of living

forever with the one who loves to life, living
the hell I gained. In freedom I cling
to this death-born life, growing in the hope
that scatters doubt's darkness by the cross's
fearsome light. The tree of death bears fruit
that rises from the grave and rests

upon all who trust His word. While no rest
remains for the wicked, there comes to the living
a boundless joy that thrives on sharing the fruit
which can't be contained; it refuses to cling
and must be shared and spread across
the world. Implanted love grows hope

that seeds the new horizon—a harvest of hope
awaits the blossoming, refusing to rest
on wilted laurels of past decay. The crossing's
complete, we've moved among the living,
no more selfish clods whose longing clings
to prides' endeavor. With hands full of fruit

that others need, one satisfied by the fruit
He's given. To newly seen neighbors, the hope
now carried reflects the one that now clings
to the heart. No longer striving, I've come to rest
in the arms of the one who loves the living
and longs to bring them to His holy cross,

and there receive the blessed burden of a cross
of their own from which buds new fruit,
new life stretching out, bringing a living
to places of darkness, shining fresh hope
that cleanses the anxious soul with the perfect rest
arriving as unsought gift. To Him we cling.

Forget the noise of star-crossed lovers with misplaced hope;
there lies the rotting fruit that gives no rest.
The place for the living is Him alone, and there we cling.

Sestina Ten

*All **blessing**, honor, thanks, and **praise***
To Father, Son, and Spirit,
*The God who **saved** us by His grace;*
*All **glory** to His merit.*
O triune God in heav'n above,
*You have revealed Your saving **love**;*
*Your blessed **name** we hallow.*

The surprising gift that longs to bless
has moved the mouth to open, to praise;
it's involuntary, can't be halted save
for the denial, rejection of the gifted glory
that belongs to Him, a votive of love
known through possessing His name.

He came from far to place His name
upon us, branding us with this blessing.
No longer our own, we live in His love
that crashed the gates to the praise
of angels cheering Him on. The wave of glory
cascaded creation as He came to save

us from ourselves—and how we needed His saving
might to rescue by the power of His name,
one so strong, containing the fullness of glory
in a single breath, a breath to bless
by forgiveness of sin. Newfound praise
rises with the reborn life of love

lived out for others, the kind of love
not found on earth. From heaven it saves
the death-bound creation now singing praise
to Him who gave all to reveal the name
of hope and salvation, the hidden blessing
breaking forth in the time that His glory

would shine forth and shatter the false glory
growing from the selfish lies lacking the love
of the creator's first embrace that blessed
the world with life. What seemed beyond saving
is made whole by the speaking of the name
that lay in the Father's heart—the one we praise

as we sing the joy, one worthy of praise,
the mystery overflowing with the glory
that fills the soul with the light of the name
gifted that we might finally know the love,
unmeasurable by the human heart, that saves.

Sing out the praise that bears the love
filled with blinding glory, that enters to save
by the might of the name that comes in blessing.

Bibliography

Ali, Agha Shahid. *Ravishing Disunities: Real Ghazals in English.* Middletown, CN: Wesleyan University Press, 2000.
Padgett, Ron. *The Teachers and Writers Handbook of Poetic Forms.* New York: Teachers and Writers Collaborative, 2000.

9 781666 773514